DIVIDE & CONQUER
BY:
KNOWLEDGE BORNE

Copyright © 2017 by William Edwards

All rights reserved. No part of this publication may be reproduced or transmitted in any form or by any means, electronic or mechanical, including photocopying and recording, or introduced into any information storage and retrieval system without the written permission of the copyright owner and the publisher of this book. Brief quotations may be used in reviews prepared for inclusion in a magazine, newspaper, or for broadcast. For further information please contact:

Knowledge Borne at IAmKnowledgeBorne@gmail.com

Cover Designer: Jamie Price

ISBN-13: 978-1981220601

ISBN-10: 1981220607

First Edition

Quantity sales: Special discounts are available on quantity purchases. Please contact the author at the e-mail address above.

DEDICATION

This book is dedicated to my people who struggle to manifest an evolutional discovery of self and live out their innate nature of divine design.

Divide & Conquer

ACKNOWLEDGEMENTS

I have to give homage to the brothers and sisters who gave their life for the advancements of the whole, the people who never accepted inferior ideologies, or allowed society to define who they were or what they would become. This book would not have been possible if I didn't have those models, some known and some not, that showed me the clandestine mental programming that submerges us on a daily basis. I give praise and great respect to the brothers and sisters that combats the niggerism that infects the ghetto, which effects the world as a whole. To all the men and women who have fell victim to the trap, the penitentiary. Never digest the image the system wants you to wear. To the people out in the streets who are lost in the whirlwind of self, I see you, I recognize you, and I hope that peace can engulf you someday. To the fallen ones who lost their life because the color of their skin or the style of their dress, know you will never be forgotten. Big shouts out to my cousins Plooky, Ru-Ru, Meisha, Brandon, Dion, Steven, Nicki, Latara, Tasha, and everybody who shows their love. Much love to my sister, my divine mother, my nieces, my lil brother, my pops, and everybody that understands what the definition of family means and represents. To my Queen, the woman who made this possible, I pay homage to you for believing in my talent and giving it the fuel to amplify my voice. To all of my supporters, I'm humbled, and I thank you for seeking out my books. Without you there will be no me. I close this out with love and much peace. Never stop fighting!

In solidarity – Knowledge Borne

TABLE OF CONTENTS

"Jails and prisons are designed to break human beings, to convert the population into specimens in a zoo – obedient to our keepers but dangerous to each other." ~ Angela Davis

INTRODUCTION

Divide and Conquer is a manifestation that grew out of ignorance, self-hatred, mis-education, and the Willie Lynch Syndrome that has corroded many minds in the ghetto. This book puts the cancerous traits, held beliefs, and programmed mind frames that have been passed down through generational pipelines under the microscope; inheritance that became more detrimental with each rebirth.

The core of this book is based around the dis-ease that has come from the teachings of the Willie Lynch Letter, which dates back to the 1700's. He brought about a course that taught other slave owners how to train the mind of Black Slaves; psychological teachings that would permanently keep them in a state of self-destruction and inferiority. This book will illuminate the fact that the techniques and systems used in his teachings are still flourishing today. It will show that the heart of his message pumps through the veins of every unconscious Black body in the present.

Willie Lynch's teachings bares its face in the foundation of street organizations (people who are terrorist and defectors to the community and race), the drug trade (a system put in place that cripples the unity and elevation of the race), pimping and prostitution (a practice that demonstrates self-hatred), and many other adverse activities. Willie Lynch understood social engineering, programming of the mind. He was able to control the minds of a group of people in generational cycles, a people who were unaware of the poisonous seeds that were being planted.

The condition the Black man, the Black woman, and the Black community are in was not an accident. It wasn't something that just happened. The Black race has been under attack since their inception in America. There has never been a time when the Black body hasn't been exploited for economic gain. White elites created an invisible force that strategically kept Blacks in a mental state of poverty, false success, desperation, hopelessness, dependency, and a subsidiarity complex. Willie Lynch, the FBI Director J. Edgar Hoover and his Counter Intelligence Program, the creators of the penal system, and many other structures implemented tactics to keep Blacks in a second-class status.

Willie Lynch focused on conquering the mind of slaves, programming it to be of benefit to him. It's the same concept of what pimps do to feeble minded women. The masses presently in the ghetto (hood niggas) are living mindlessly, unconscious of their enslaved state. The Black community was purposely broken, and it stems back to the days of slavery with white men who formulated a plan to keep Blacks in a permanent mental condition of enslavement, a condition that would be inherited to their offspring.

Most people can't even fathom that such mental engineering is possible and took place, but it's very simple. Take a pimp who mentally trains his woman to be submissive. If he catches that woman while she's young and gets deep enough in her mind everything that she does will be a branch of him. Once she has offspring she will only be able to teach them what she knows, the seeds that the pimp planted in her head. The offspring will be in an unhealthier state than his or her mother because they are the first generation to be born with only the teachings of the pimp. The cycle will continue with their offspring until the pimp's teachings will be the only thing they know.

Now think about it on a much grandiose scale, slavery. A pimp's manipulation is miniscule compared to that of a slave master. The slave master stripped away his slaves' humanity, culture, and identity. While at the same time molding the slaves' mind to be feeble and menial. This process started from the day of their birth, and for a lot of them it didn't end until the day of their death. The offspring of those slaves only had understanding of what was taught to their parents, which was self-hatred, distrust amongst their own, dependency on whites, and the superiority of the white race.

Slave masters used religion, one of the most powerful and manipulative tools ever, to justify the status and cruel treatment of Blacks. God was used to bring about submission and fear within the subconscious of the Black race to submit to the false superiority claim of the white race. They taught that Black skin was a curse from God, and that their status as slaves were divinely justified. *Ephesians 6:5* was a scripture that was instilled in slaves to make them obedient. It states, *"Slaves, obey your earthly masters with deep respect and fear. Serve them sincerely as you would serve Christ. Try to please them all the time, not just when they are watching you. As slaves of Christ, do the will of God with all your heart. Work with enthusiasm, as though you were working for the Lord rather than for people. Remember that the*

Lord will reward each one of us for the good we do, whether we are slaves or free." The Bible was a tool that was used to make the minds of slaves docile to their inhumane condition. They even trained them with a picture of a white man to depict God, putting it in the Black mind the omnipotence of white skin.

In the infamous Willie Lynch Letter, he spoke on the importance of creating distrust and envy amongst Blacks. He trained them to be suspicious and envious of other Black people, creating a destructive wedge of division. Every characteristic that was different amongst Blacks he taught to irradiate them, the shades of their skin (dark-skin, light-skin), their age (young, old), their sex (males, females), their education, and many other distinctions that have caused separation within the race. This indoctrination created a prejudicial mind frame that is still around today. In the present we fight each other because of what we have been taught to believe are differences amongst us, instead of uniting against the forces that are destroying us.

On the James River in 1712 Willie Lynch educated his counterparts that they must distrust Blacks because they were savages, but told them that it was necessary that Blacks completely trust, honor, and depend solely on them. Not much has changed from then until now in that aspect. Blacks, especially Black men, are the most distrustful people to walk the earth in the eyes of other ethnic groups. The economic position of the Black race is in a depended state. The food we eat comes from white-owned farms and grocery stores. The housing we live in are owned by whites (banks and mortgage companies). The corporations we work for are owned by whites, and the government system we depend on was built by racist whites, and is run by covert racists in the present. We are an ethnic group of consumers who don't own anything, which makes us the easiest group of people to be exploited.

People believe we can cure the terminal cancer of slave mental engineering that have corroded Black brains for over 300 years with community centers, actionless prayer, basketball programs, job programs, money, and other surface treatments that don't restore health to the core malfunction at hand, the mind. The condition the Black race is in can only be corrected by looking at the Genesis of the problem that was programmed into the minds of our ancestors, genealogically traveling the pipeline to the present. By not analyzing and curing the source people will forever be unconsciously imprisoned by the Willie Lynch Syndrome.

The content in this book is a direct attack on all the lopsided ideologies that we have embraced as truth, the pride in being a hood nigga, the false honor and power of street organizations, the distrust and suspicion amongst each other, and many other deleterious beliefs that have molded a race on the verge of self-annihilation. It's time to start analyzing the heart of the problem, the materialization of the Willie Lynch Syndrome....

Divide & Conquer

CHAPTER 1:
THE CREATION OF THE GHETTO

THE GHETTO

Exactly what is a ghetto, and what is its function in the society of America? A ghetto is a section of a city, a thick populated slum that's inhibited by a minority group that is socially and economically restricted. The minority group is categorized as niggas; Black people who are economically, politically, and socially disenfranchised. The ghetto was constructed to keep a people, Black people, in a state of despair, desolation, wretchedness, and hopelessness. It is a dump off for the people in America that are not wanted, the underclass.

The ghetto was meant to breed ineptitude, malfunction, despondency, and a group of people who were broken. They are areas that have been excluded from the operations of American society and left by the wayside to wither away in the ashes of poverty and chaos. The social restrictions of the people who are confined in the ghetto were put into place to keep Blacks in a demoralized state, just like in the days of slavery. The ghetto is the grandchild of slavery, but more detrimental because the bodies are no longer enslaved, it's the minds that have been captured.

Economically the ghetto is a place that is capitalized off of from every angle. Liquor stores pollute the hood with alcohol and expired D grade food. Clothing stores sell knock-offs at retail prices. Planned Parenthood exterminates droves of Black babies a year. The Justice System has made billions of dollars off the backs of incarcerated Blacks, and many other entities that strip Black communities. Money flows out of the hood in abundance, Black dollars, but none of that cash ever comes back. That's why there are dilapidated buildings and houses, outdated schools that are failing the children, scarce employment opportunities, and Black bodies that are being exploited in every way possible. The Arabs, Europeans, Asians, and unconscious Blacks (drug dealers, pimps, stick-up kids, etc.) are all manipulating the Black race to put a dollar in their pocket.

People who are brainwashed are in a state of survival. They will do drastic things to keep their head above water. Drug dealing, killing each other to get ahead, exploitation (believing that's how they have to eat), sexual slavery (prostitution), and many other things that keeps the community as a whole in a state of niggerism. The actions of a few is what keeps the cancerous functions of the ghetto operative; that was the plan of the Willie Lynch theory.

Willie Lynch instructed his peers to instill in their slaves a will to never want to aspire to be anything more than a slave. He taught them to be complacent with the condition they lived in, physically and mentally. He trained them to never believe they deserved anything more in life than to be a nigga. In the present, those teachings are still strong in the minds of Black males and Black females who are contaminated by the Willie Lynch Syndrome. They love the ghetto, being socially excluded, taking pride in being a 'hood nigga', and living out the teachings that Willie Lynch instilled in the mental DNA of the Black race.

The function of the ghetto has worked out perfectly in some respects for the people who constructed it. It has created dependent mentalities (government assistance programs, food stamps, low-income housing). It made the mind impoverished and blinded to a genocidal existence. The hood was built on the foundation of self-destruction, a mechanism that reincarnates itself with each generation that comes. You have to ask yourself, how did the state of the Black community get to the point of ignorance, self-hatred, violence, corruption, and destruction?

THE ATTACK ON THE GHETTO

In the past, during the peak of the Black Power Movement, the mid-sixties into the seventies, the Black community had strong ties of unification. There were bonds of brotherhood and sisterhood, Black grocery stores, Black clothing stores, Black insurance companies, Black banks, Black colleges, and many other Black enterprises. They came together and held each other accountable, because they understood that the actions of a few represented many.

Black people of the past became aware that they couldn't look without to become empowered, they had to look within. Black Power and Black Consciousness built a strong momentum that seemed like it couldn't be stopped. Black people were becoming proud to be Black. They understood that in order to elevate in America they would have to do it themselves, and all across the country Black communities were transitioning into cultural economic communities.

As Blacks gained power in the political and business sector, the establishment took notice of the climate that was happening in the country with the Black race. They were gaining the knowledge of their beauty and divinity, which in the eyes of the oppressors were awakening a threat to National Security (white people). To them an educated Black person who loved him or herself was dangerous, which meant they had to be annihilated. There has never been a time in the history of this country where we have not been under oppressive attack, whether out in the open or done covertly.

During the epoch of Black elevation a few death blows were in the works. A team called the Counter Intelligence Program that was run by the head of the FBI, Director J. Edgar Hoover, was being borne. Alongside the Counter Intelligence Program was the illusion of equality with the passing of the Civil Rights Act in 1964, a Bill that destroyed the monetary unity within the Black community. Then came Richard Nixon with the birth of his declaration to restore 'Law and Order', which was code words to put the Black race back in its place of crippleness. After these events were set into motion, a tsunami of drugs and guns flooded the ghetto. This brought about a new economy for gangs and street niggas. The hands that built the platform of destruction sat back and watched Blacks kill each other off mentally and physically over drugs, blocks, colors, and an array of other things that destroyed unity.

THE COUNTER INTELLIGENCE PROGRAM

The platform that was set moved a lot of Blacks' mentality from Black pride/Black empowerment to pride in image, materials, drugs, and human trafficking. They traded their dignity, integrity, morals and respect for money. The United States Government introduced a false image of power to them, the street nigga. One of the many turncoats in the ghetto, because they are willing to sell out their own race just to look like they have gotten ahead or are of importance. They are the destroyers of elevation. J. Edgar Hoover understood that they could be used to further his objective, destruction of Black consciousness and intelligence, keeping the Black race infected by the Willie Lynch Syndrome.

J. Edgar Hoover was one of the most powerful men in the nation during his heydays, and his Counter Intelligence Program was a bloodline to Willie Lynch's teachings. His attack on Black people and the ghetto they resided in was more detrimental than slave owners of the past because he took the lessons from Willie Lynch and intensified them. He ignited a deep-rooted distrust, envy, hatred, and mental segregation within the Black race. He also brought new elements to the equation: drugs, money, and gangs. He illuminated division and knew street gangs would be the perfect avenue to create chaos, Black genocide.

Hoover attacked the Black race from all sides - mentally, emotionally, and physically (the assassination of *Fred Hampton*, the Chicago chapter leader of the Black Panthers, *Malcom X*, a leader in the Nation of Islam, and many others). He placed disrupters in the ghetto

(Black men and Black women who were turncoats) who brought about strife and dissention.

The Counter Intelligence Program attacked any group that built on Black elevation from the inside out, crumbling the foundation. Cowards and traders like William O'Neil, Fred Hampton's security guard and the person who set-up his murder by the Chicago Police Department. Any man or woman who fell under the *"Black Messiah"* cloth was either neutralized (made ineffective, nullified), imprisoned like the Black Power Movement activist *Angela Davis, Assata Shakur, Geronimo Pratt, Mumia Abu Jamal,* or killed.

The Counter Intelligence Program polluted the ghetto with separatist ideologies, materialistic mind frames, and built an aura of hatred for progression. Once division was put into place amongst the Black Power Movement in came the drugs and guns flooding cities like Chicago, New York, Los Angeles, and many others. The drug trade brought about a false sense that a person in the ghetto could live the American dream: money, cars, clothes – the finer things in life. What was the trade off? A new business machine for Black bodies, prisons and the destruction of the Black community by Black people through drugs, violence, terror, and exploitation.

THE SMOKESCREEN OF CIVIL RIGHTS

The Civil Rights Movement was powerful, but it also created cracks in the foundation of the Black community. A small fraction of people benefited, but the majority sunk into an underclass. The Civil

Rights Movement strived to gain practical equality (being able to sit next to white people, shop in their stores, ride their buses, and many other things that people thought was some kind of honor), and not economic equality.

The passing of the Civil Rights Bill caused droves of Blacks to abandon spending their money in the Black community. This behavior left neighborhoods neglected because Blacks were so anxious to spend their hard-earned money with people who hated their existence. This is still in practice today.

The Civil Rights Bill brought about the changing of the little money that Blacks did have. This created a catastrophic blow against Black elevation. It brought about an underclass that went into a deeper hole of debt and hopelessness, while whites became richer off their monies. In the present nothing has changed. Everybody still exploits the Black body, even Black people. This is why the economy in the ghetto is nonexistent; the reason why we are in a state of economic, mental, emotional, and spiritual recession.

When desegregation took place a lot of Blacks falsely believed White products were better than Black products, the blinding of White purity. Instead of continuing to grow as producers, employers, and owners we became content as consumers. We became a people who looked of value, but had no true wealth behind us. The ghetto in this moment is infected with this lopsided mentality to look of importance, but to be irrelevant in reality.

A lot of Black minds are consumed with materials that companies have trained them to believe are of value; designer clothes, rims, foreign cars, and many other fake displays of wealth and success. Society has brainwashed people, especially Black people, that valueless materials will make them important.

The Civil Rights Bill brought about an illusion of progress, a backend form of equality that siphoned money from the Black community instead of equally spreading it out. Black people turned their backs on the growth of their own neighborhoods and businesses to unconsciously help build other peoples' economies. Arab, White, and Asian communities became wealthier while the Black race fell into a state of dependency and extreme poverty. It's very similar to the slave who worked all his or her life just to give it over to the slave owner. There's really no difference in today's age and time except we willingly do it.

THE CODED ASSAIL

Along with Hoover's attack, the illusion of equality (the Civil Rights Bill), in came the order from the Commander in Chief to bring back 'Law and Order'. What did this mean? If the only group that was considered unlawful and dangerous in the nation were Black, who were they talking about? That declaration was coded for White America that the Nixon administration would put Blacks back in their place of inferiority. How would this be done? The penal system. Hoover would flood the Black community with drugs and guns. This would create crime. The United States Government would then step in and get down on the states to lock up the offenders. This was a new form of enslavement, the felon. Once the felon was released from his or her confinement, society could then deny them jobs, dignity, and ignore their humanity, just like the slave.

Former President Nixon was a camouflager who appealed to Black America by showing he was in support of their causes and struggles. However, what he was really doing was under handing the Black race with his 'Law and Order'. This was the starting point of the prison industrial complex. Black men were being hoarded into prisons like Africans were hoarded onto slave ships in the past. It was colorblind to the American citizen which made it almost impossible to contest that the Black race was being targeted. In the eyes of the people they only saw the criminal.

The establishment understood that blatant racism was being condemned in America, and that that institution was a dying breed. So they switched from going off of color to going off of titles – the criminal, the felon, the prostitute, the gangbanger, the killer, the drug dealer, the pimp, the drug addict became a false depiction of the Black man and Black woman. This image became so prevalent that even Black people started believing the lies that were being programmed in the minds of White America about them.

Being a felon excluded a large number of Blacks from participating in the liberties of being an American citizen, the same position slaves were in because they were slaves. It became easy to discriminate against the Black race once they were placed in the status of the miscreant criminal, and the public believed it was colorblind. People weren't treating people who had been incarcerated harshly because of their skin color; it was because they were felons. Black bodies started being hoarded into correctional institutions (reformed slave plantations) at alarming rates because they saw that there wouldn't be many to contest the new enslavement of Blacks (criminals). The comparisons are undisputable between the slave and the felon.

The soul of Willie Lynch is present and breaths through the lungs of people who try and destroy Black progress, the architects of the ghetto. The condition a large number of Blacks reside in was not a coincidence. The ghetto was peppered with liquor stores (selling toxins to keep Blacks blinded to reality), Planned Parenthood (a business that has ended the life of millions of Black babies), Rent-A-Centers, Payday Loan Stores (predatory lenders who exploit poor Blacks by keeping them confined to a lifetime of debt) for a reason. All of these entities have been put into place to make money off the plight of Black people. Then add drugs, guns, no job opportunities, failing schools, and a lack of correct guidance, you create an underclass of hopelessness.

Everything in the ghetto was setup to keep the Black race in a desperate state of inferiority, blind to the potential that resides within them. The condition of the Black community has a lineage that goes back hundreds of years. Blacks were and still are attacked from every angle: mentally (failing schools and households), physically (prisons, Black on Black violence, police brutality), emotionally (toxic mental instability), spiritually (slave religions that teach Black minds to be servants, slave to a white depiction), and institutionally (racist policies through the banks, mortgage companies, and insurance companies). The sad part is in the present the niggas and hood niggas are the Black race's most eminent threat. They have the minds of racist whites. White people don't have to get their hands dirty anymore because they taught the niggas to be their spitting image, keeping the hood completely operative.

Divide & Conquer

CHAPTER 2:
THE MAKING OF THE N****

THE N****

The ghetto as we learned is a thickly populated slum that is inhabited by minority groups that are socially and economically restricted. Who is this minority group? In the eyes of the white elite and poor whites they are characterized as niggas, which is a person who is economically, politically, and socially disenfranchised, Black people. Both the ghetto and the nigga were a creation that worked perfectly for people like Willie Lynch, because Black people have embraced both as a badge of endearment. A large majority of Black people have chosen to be niggas, are willing to die for their hood (the ghetto), love the lessons that were passed down to them from slave owners.

Willie Lynch and slave masters all across the United States instilled in their slaves a will to never want to aspire to be anything more than a slave. He taught to program in them a high level of contentment that was passed down to their offspring, which caused them to live in the mental state of a slave. They viewed the world through the eyes of a slave. In the present, it's no different. There are niggas in the ghetto that don't want anything more than to be niggas in the ghetto (chasing crumbs, riding rims, encouraging Black women to exploit themselves, dressing fresh, and being the Brickman), mentally enslaved in generational cycles unable to rise to their true purpose.

The way a street nigga operates clearly shows the effects of the Willie Lynch Syndrome. He wanted slaves to be parasites to their own, and the street nigga is that parasite that eats away at the Black race's elevation and progress. Willie Lynch taught that slaves must see the differences amongst each other, that they must distrust one another. He created this division through alienation of skin colors, gender, body physique, the side of town they lived on, the texture of their hair, intelligence, and many other aspects.

Right now, in this moment, the practice of separation is still alive in the hearts of people who are infected with the Willie Lynch Syndrome. In the ghetto people create division amongst each other because of skin color, the block they live on, the color they wear, foolish gang creed, the city they're from, the era they were born in, and many other detachments. We are perishing in the streets because of this illusion of differences within the race. This concept brings about a 'fuck them other niggas' mentality, and is the father of gangs and organizations.

Willie Lynch stated that after creating a nigga mind frame it shall carry on and will become self-refueling and self-generating for hundreds, maybe thousands of years. His prediction is a reality for the Black race. White people don't need to lynch, castrate, burn, terrorize, or kill us anymore, because they have trained the niggas very well how to be the oppressors. They are flooding the Black community with poison (drugs), stepping on the necks of their own believing it is necessary to get ahead. They are murdering other Black people over blocks and gang stupidity that serves no purpose to elevation. The infected unconscious Black man and woman are bringing about degradation to the Black race through their ignorance of self.

Who falls under the category of a nigga? Any person who is affected by the Willie Lynch Syndrome. Any person who brings about disunity, senseless violence, and terrorize the community in which they stay. The males and females who pass down detrimental beliefs to their offspring (get money by any means necessary, teaching them that they will never rise above the hood). A nigga is any Black person who hinders the elevation of the race, the dudes and females who are selling drugs, destroying the core of their people just to get paid. The sissy adult boys who disrespect the womb by encouraging women to sell their bodies, and the mentally dead dudes who run around killing off brothers and sisters pleasing the minds of racist whites who find joy in our plight.

THE SELLOUT

A nigga is a pure definition of a sellout, because they will sell, trade, and step on the necks of their own to get ahead. Out in the streets they sell out their people on a daily basis (sell drugs to them, pimp them out, rob them, etc.) to wear designer clothes, ride slick, and have crumbs in their pocket believing it's success.

Willie Lynch taught his slaves to abandon who they were, forgetting their culture, their values, their morals, their dignity, and respect. He trained them to look at themselves as savages and beasts.

In today's time, there are males who proudly proclaim savage life, or that they are beasts, living out the mental engineering that took place hundreds of years ago.

In the present, people don't see, nor do they understand the idiocy in titling themselves niggas, goons, savages, and other self-inflicting names that they live out. The irony that there are Black people who take these terms that were handed down from slave masters and try to beautify them is mind blowing. At the end of the day, the titles represent the same thing they did 300 years ago. People understand that words have power, and what the power activates is how you view yourself. If you believe that you are a nigga, a savage, or a beast then you are going to live in that nature just like the white man taught you.

The mind is supreme, and Willie Lynch understood the power they could hold over slaves if they captured and programmed their minds. However, the mind has the innate ability to correct and re-correct itself over a period of time if it can reconnect with a substantial cultural base. So, what they did was erase the slaves' mental history, and created a multiplicity of phenomena of illusions, a nigga, a savage, a beast. This false reality of self was then passed down from generation to generation, creating people that were proud to represent these titles.

Willie Lynch also manufactured the reversal of roles when it came to the slave woman and man. He taught the woman to become the head and the man to become the liability to the family structure. He taught to engrain in slave men a weakness and a dependent nature, which is evident in today's time. A lot of males have become the emotional unstable factor in the unit of the family. They live off their woman, stay in her house, drive her car, and exist in the mind frame of a dependent child.

The nigga is an emotionally unstable being that acts first and thinks second. The evidence is clear in cities like Chicago, Detroit, and Milwaukee of males who are temperamentally unbalanced. When a person can go out and shoot another person over a dispute he is emotional. When the first solution in the midst of an argument is to fight, a person is emotionally fragile. Niggas are more emotional than females; the only difference is they are more prone to do violence.

Black males have taken on an incorrect image of manhood, which is the Sambo nigga (a Black male that is mentally weak and dependent, but physically strong). A large number of Black males are existing in a machismo state of mind. They believe that getting money, riding customized whips, having sex with an abundance of females, and wearing designer clothes is a representation of manhood. They equate knowing how to fight, being tough and fearless with characteristics of a man, which in reality are the traits of the Sambo nigga.

In the present, the nigga is promoted to the youth through a multitude of avenues. Unconscious parents teach niggerism in the household. Most rap music reinforces it's cool and acceptable to be dumb and foolish as long as you have money. The television networks depict Blacks in a negative light, and so do many other streams of media. White people who are aware of the social engineering that took place, and is still taking place, sit back and laugh at the stupidity of Black people who gracefully accept being a nigga.

The nigga was not created because of race, but for economic value. In Willie Lynch's letter he pointed out that once a slave master broke a nigga he or she was ready for a long life of sound and efficient work and the reproduction of a unit of good labor force. Black slaves were the driving force that made America wealthy, yet all the money that was made off of their backs went into the pockets of the white elite. An abundance of whites became generationally rich off of slavery, and right now in this moment nothing has changed except the names. The new slave is the street nigga, the inmate, the goon.

Not much has changed from then until now. Big money is still being made off of the backs of Blacks. The slave plantations have transformed into prison compounds and ghetto compounds. Niggas in the streets are being pimped out in the rawest fashion, because at the end of their run the government will have everything that they grinded for, risked their life for. Plus, they will take part of their life and make a profit off of their confined body.

A nigga has a destructive mind frame. They unconsciously hate themselves, which was the plan, making it easy to hate and destroy their own. This image and belief disconnected them from the race, which made them able to sell drugs to Black people, pimp, degrade, and disrespect Black women. It made them able to glorify killing Black bodies, and exploit their own in a race to falsely get ahead by acquiring cheap materials that are sold to them as if they had value. The mind of the nigga is captured in an impressionable, zombie like state, and whoever is around them can control it.

RESPONSIBILITY

In order to live in your natural state, the nigga inside of you must die, and the Black man or Black woman must be born. What is a Black man or a Black woman? A lot of people think it's the color of their skin but fail to realize there are many niggas with Black skin that does not represent the Black race (gang members, pimps, drug pushers, prostitutes, etc.). A Black person is a being of great respect who has knowledge of self, knowledge of community, morals, honor, and principles. He or she is a person who is culturally conscious to the struggle, sensible in his or her actions, dependable, and reliable. It is a man, woman, or child that adds to the community, and adds to the race as a whole.

Being an upright Black man or Black woman comes with a deep responsibility to the people, which is how societies (the Black community) thrives and prospers. The Jews are a prime example of a disparaged group of people who bonded together and rose above the ugliness of their history. They were a people who were forced into the ghetto in Europe, which is where the term comes from. They were a people who were exploited, attacked, and treated in an inferior manner. They were hoarded into concentration camps during World War II and slaughtered like animals. They were burnt in pits, put into gas chambers, but yet they never laid down and accepted the position their oppressors wanted them to remain in.

Divide & Conquer

The Jewish people rose up because they held members of their group accountable. They supported each other, they spent their money with each other, and made sure they progressed instead of regressed. They only make up around 0.2% of the world's population and 2% of the American population, yet they have become one of the most powerful groups in the world. They are major owners of large revolutionary corporations in media, sports, cinema, etc. They are one of the wealthiest groups in the world, mentally and materially because they understood unity and community preservation.

So, why is the Black race, which is much larger in numbers, in a state of stagnation, a state of regression and self-enslavement? There is a magnitude of reasons, but the nucleus is the Willie Lynch Syndrome. The nigga mind frame must be eradicated for the Black man, woman, and child to be born. A renaissance of Black cultural empowerment must be manifested in the minds of the infected, and an intellectual cultivation of self needs to occur to bring the infected back to his or her natural state.

CHAPTER 3:
THE DESTRUCTION OF THE BLACK WOMAN

THE FETUS

Willie Lynch paid much attention to the position the Black woman held as a slave, because he understood the supreme position she played in the generational training of the Black mind. How can people control the mind of a race in a generational cycle? As Willie Lynch outlined in his teachings that the person doing the breaking of the slave should pay little attention to the generation that was originally broke but concentrate on the future generations; corrupting the fetus in the womb. This process can only be done by breaking the mother, which in turn will teach her offspring in its early years of development the self-destructing belief system that was taught to her.

This cycle of brokenness will be self-refueling and self-generating for hundreds of years until a generation becomes conscious to the toxic mis-education that was planted in their ancestral mental make-up. If a person has been trained since the womb to be a nigga, he or she don't know his or her true self or position as a Black man or Black woman. This disconnection makes it impossible to break the mental chains that enslave them, and so it continues on once they have offspring. This practice is still alive in this moment because people with a hood nigga mentality raises a child with the same mind frame.

In his teachings Willie Lynch highlighted the importance of reversing the roles of the Black woman and the Black man. Going off the Law of Nature a woman has a healthy dependency on the males in her life (her father, her brother, her partner). Men are protectors and providers by nature. However, Willie Lynch taught to eliminate those natural characteristics from the equation. Reversing the roles left Black women unsupported, with the image of the Black man completely destroyed (hood niggas, dope boys, pimps, gangsters, and other ugly characteristics).

The distortion of the Black male's image brought about a switch in the minds of Black women from a healthy psychological dependent state to a destructive independent state. The woman became the provider and protector. In order for a people to elevate they must understand their interconnection and interdependency to one another. With the Black male out of his natural role he becomes a liability to the cultural community, which is what Willie Lynch aimed for. He strived to create the 'nigga' who had no respect, no honor, or admiration for the womb which they came. They were programmed to depend solely upon the woman (their mothers, sisters, partners) because they were unable to stand on their own due to the mis-education of their innate position.

This mental engineering has brought about generations of weak, pathetic males who depend on women as their hustle and livelihood; grown boys who need their momma or woman to buy their clothes, feed them, give them money, and many other boyish things because they never reached the development stage of walking into manhood. For some this process seems impossible because they lack the proper tools that are supposed to be handed down during the transition from boyhood to manhood.

Willie Lynch knew the mothers were the key piece to accomplish the mental engineering of the offspring. He taught slave owners to psychologically train their slaves to be content with being slaves, and they handed that same training down to their babies. They taught boys to be mentally weak and dependent, but physically strong. This brought about boys who are emotionally unstable and only able to think in the physical, fighting and causing harm because they don't have it in them to solve problems with their mind. Violence is their only outlet, which is evident out in the streets.

OBJECTIFIED

In the history of America, the Black woman has been the most abused being on the earth. She has been bred like a dog, sold as a concubine, beat, branded, and degraded in the purest form by whites and some of her own. The nigga was taught to embrace the practices of the white man towards the Black woman. He was taught to disrespect the Black womb, which is the same as disrespecting one's self being that the womb is the first home of all civilization. He was taught to look at the Black woman as ugly, subservient, a piece of property, which made it impossible to have respect for her.

Divide & Conquer

The practice of disrespecting women, especially Black women is so strong and prevalent in today's time. Even Black women degrade and belittle other Black women because of the color of their skin, the texture of their hair, their education, and an array of other things. Unconscious Black women have accepted the notion that their value is in their booty and breasts. It's in the kind of handbag they carry, or the designer shoes on their feet. Some rap music places the woman in a category of an object. She is only something of pleasure, a piece of property, just like slave masters viewed her in the times of slavery. She was a bitch who money could be made off of, and a piece of pussy he could fuck on.

The nigga is the embodiment of the white slave master when it comes to how he treats the Black woman. In today's time they have a term that is eerie, and deeply embraced called 'breaking a bitch'. This means taking her for everything that she has, making her submissive. The scary similarity is that Willie Lynch pointed out the importance of 'breaking a bitch' in his letter. He said, "If she (the Black woman) shows any signs of resistance in submitting completely to your will, do not hesitate to use the bullwhip on her to extract the last bit of bitch out of her. Take care not to kill her, for in doing so, you spoil good economies."

Think about that for a moment...The Black woman meant nothing more to the slave owner than good economies (one's personal resource of money). There is no difference from a pimp who prostitutes a woman for a personal resource of money, a dude who swindles a woman for personal resource of money, or a slave owner who used Black women for a personal resource of money. What's the difference between the nigga who would sellout his people for economic gain and a slave owner who sold Blacks for economic gain? The Black male of today who has the Willie Lynch Syndrome wears the ideological shoes of the slave master and uses the exact same practices towards Black women.

DEFINED

A person cannot deny the vital essence of the woman who has knowledge of herself and walks in her wisdom. The woman is the first person every human being on this earth connected with. While in the womb your livelihood depended on her. For most, once you are birthed she is the person who nurtures your growth and development. She is our first teacher if she is conscious to her position. However, a lot of Black males and Black females have forgotten that divine essence because it has been muddied. It has been replaced by the acceptance of being a bitch, a hoe, living savage life, and many other corrosions that continuously erodes the Black foundation.

Through the training that was engrained in the minds of Black people an unconsciousness of self-hatred was born. Women were given the definition of what beauty meant, and so they covered their natural self with paint, hid their natural hair with weave, injected their butt and breasts, and an array of other self-hating practices. They started living out the insecurities that were programmed in their minds by white people who gave them the definition of what beauty represented. In today's time the only difference is it's done through consumerism.

Clothing companies, shoe companies, make-up companies, car companies, and many other entities tell people what beauty is.

Some Black women have embraced the toxic false beliefs about themselves, and now live in the present of objectivity. They are only about their asses, hair, and clothes; feeling as if they have nothing else to offer. They have become so blind to their divinity and the fact that they are the mothers of the universe that they don't even require or demand respect. They have reached a depressing point in time where they accept pseudo-men who step out on them, drain them of their money, and degrade them in the purest form. Yet, they hold on passionately to these inadequate pseudo-men because the value of self is nonexistent due to insecurities of detrimental generational engineering.

The Black woman not living in her natural state of divinity has created a culture of young boys and adult boys to have no respect for the womb, or the essence of the Black woman. They only see her in the light of a bitch, a hoe, or something to fuck on. It has created a culture of young girls and adult girls who follow in the footsteps of what they were taught; a culture of females who disrespect their mind, their body, and their soul. What is the end result? A race that is lost in a chaotic existence.

Everything that we hold to be true, the way we view women, the way women view themselves, and the way we view the world are learned systems. Ask yourself who taught you to look at women as bitches and hoes? When you find that out then ask yourself who taught them, and continue to go back until you reach the source. A starting point that will be traced back to racist white men in a racist country. You do not respect yourself if you disrespect the Black woman or encourage her to live in her lower self.

The Black race has been mentally tricked to turn on each other, hate each other, kill each other, degrade each other, and it's done through the destruction of the Black woman. By polluting the minds of the mothers of our civilization they have molded every mind that comes from that womb. They created niggas, bitches, hoes, and savages who are inferior, mentally weak, dependent and unable to stand on his or her own. The facts cannot be contested because the proof of the Willie Lynch Syndrome is right in our faces in every ghetto across this country.

REBUILT

The Black woman, your mother, your daughter, your sister must be supported and rebuilt in the natural image of her divinity. Recognize her beauty being that you are from that womb, show her by your actions as an upright man that she is not a hoe, a thot, a jumper, or whatever other ignorant term is placed on Black queens who lack the true knowledge of what they are and who they are.

As men, our women are supposed to be a reflection of us, respectable, honorable, and upright. Become a vanguard for the Black race, instead of the weak ass nigga that's helping the destruction of us. Peace is the highest elevation of love, and it's time for a movement of

Black love. A love so strong that it will annihilate the self-hatred, the ignorance, and the brainwashing of the Black mind.

How do you start this self-movement? By simply caring about the words that come out of your mouth. Speak out when you know there is an injustice. Educate yourself so you can teach the generation under you to care about their actions. It starts with you to bring about change within your community. To encourage a woman to live in her lower self is to cripple a generation.

CHAPTER 4:
THE IDIOCY OF GANGS

FALSE POWERS

In cities all across the country Black males and Black females recede deeper in Willie Lynch's grand scheme of divide and conquer through the creation of street gangs and street organizations. These entities have placed Black communities in a blindness state of violence, ignorance, hatred, and a compliance to the teachings of Willie Lynch. He stated, "I assure you that distrust is stronger than trust, and envy is stronger than adulation, respect or admiration." He understood that envy and distrust created division, and division brought about a weak bond within the community and race.

People like Willie Lynch planted seeds in the minds of our ancestors, and we took the seeds and nurtured them, allowing them to grow into a forest of niggerism. We pay homage to him and his teachings every time we pick up a pack, pimp out and degrade a woman, create separation within the stupidity of organizations and block claiming, or are willing to step on the necks of people in exchange for materials.

Gangs and organizations are the blueprint of what the Willie Lynch concept aimed to accomplish. Teach them how to be niggas, intellectually retarded, dependent, but physically strong. Gangs are toxic organisms of false brotherhood and sisterhood that operate in a mindless existence with no true purpose. They are terminal cancer to Black elevation and community elevation, yet for some idiotic reason young and older males continue to keep these death traps alive by joining them. Why is this?

Street gangs, which formed into organizations, were born in the ghettos of places like New York City, Chicago, Los Angeles, and many other cities by kids who had a void in them. Kids who lacked a feeling of importance, self-worth, and self-esteem. So instead of becoming a person of true esteem they created an illusion, organizations. They gave their gangs supreme titles and symbols, set positions up like royal empires (kings, princes, chiefs, etc.), but held no real power. These kids yearned to be recognized as a somebody, whether through fear or false respect.

Organizations constructed a fairytale of supremacy in their heads with meaningless colors, numbers, symbols, and sayings. They marketed this fake aura to other boys and girls who were mentally weak and needed to be accepted. They took on elite titles like Black Disciples, Vice Lords, Peace Stone Rangers, and an array of other names. Yet, everything they stood for was based around violence, corruption, and chaos masked in the fake positivity of creed. Hypocrites in the purest form because they weren't disciples who brought peace to the Black community. They were niggas, race traders, masquerading around like they were upright and righteous.

INDOCTRINATION

Gang indoctrination is no different than slave masters indoctrinating their slaves. Both the gang leader and slave master controlled the way the people under their rule operated through fear and structure. If they didn't completely submit to the indoctrination then they would have to face the consequences, punishments, and violations (beatings). Both the gang leader and the slave master taught their slave to hate themselves (by hating their own). In gangs, other Black men and Black women are oppositions if they wear a different color, live on a different block, use different symbols, and an array of other moronic things. Slave masters' teachings were similar in nature because they understood the power of division.

The majority of people who join gangs do so because they are weak minded and insecure. They are unconscious of self and their full potential. They need to be accepted by the people around them or in their neighborhood that possess a fake sense of power. Gangs live off of delusional images of importance. They create fear and gain fictitious respect through intimidation tactics, just like slave masters did. They do horrendous things to instill fear within the people around them. They do this so a person will never contest or disobey the order of the gang. They are no different than groups like the Klu Klux Klan who followed the same blueprint.

BY YOUR OWN

There is no question that since the beginning of the Black race's bondage in America we have been under attack, however, in the present the Black race is not only under attack by every other race (Whites, Arabs, Asians), but by its own through the foolishness of gangs, a group of misguided niggas who are parasites to the elevation of the race. In the present you don't only have to worry about the racist practices of the country. You have to worry about the Black male standing next to you who might blow your brains out for the watch on your wrist.

You have to think, why would a person join a group that anybody can get in? It takes no requirements, except being a sendoff, to be a gangbanger or part of an organization. Unconscious males align themselves with the lowest grade of people who prosper to become losers. In the history of time there has never been a person who can say being a Gangster Disciple, a Vice Lord, a Black Stone, or whatever has advanced them in finding peace in their life, being successful in a spiritual, emotional, or mental state. Gangs don't bring success or prosperity. So why would you join it or be a part of it?

Being affiliated does not represent manhood or womanhood – you are only going to find that within, not without. Embracing the ideology of ignorance, corruption, and separation shows a lack thereof of manhood and womanhood. You have to think about it and ask yourself why would you follow behind and honor males who have caused chaos within generations of people and failed in life? *Larry*

Hoover, Jeff Fort, David Barksdale, Boonie Black, Mickey Cogwell, Willie Lorde, and many others have added nothing to the people they governed. The only thing they brought about was death, destruction, drugs, division, and confusion of self. They were malignant to the race, yet they are praised like they were honorable men.

The gang leaders that I named are some of the role models that are looked up to in the ghetto. Generations that are inspiring to be locked up or popped up, following in the same footsteps of males who taught the teachings of Willie Lynch to millions of impressionable girls and boys; black bodies that have perished in the streets for a purposeless ideology and cause. Kids and mindless adults are out in the streets willing to give their life for colors, symbols, hand gestures, and other stupid shit for the love of a gang or organization that doesn't give a fuck about them.

TURNCOATS

When you think about it, gang members and niggas are the true definition of race traders, sellouts, and the ghetto understanding of an Uncle Tom because they have completely turned their back on Black elevation, which is self-elevation. Anytime a Black person is willing to push drugs in the community, pimp out women, rob their people, or terrorize the community they are sellouts because they are willing to trade off their own in exchange for bankrolls in their pockets or an overpriced vehicle. These Uncle Tom sellout niggas (drug dealers, pimps, gang members, robbers, etc.) will sell their soul to look the part of importance.

The unconscious Blacks that plague the ghetto are only for self. If they have to kill, pollute and destroy their own just to get ahead they are in agreement with it. Willie Lynch said, "it is necessary that your slaves (Black people) trust and depend on us. They must love, respect, and only trust us." That's present right now in this moment. There is a large number of Black people in the ghetto who only love, respect, and trust in the dollar, which is a representation of the white man. Niggas will pimp out a woman for the dollar, kill other Black people for the dollar, sell drugs for the dollar, and many other ill-hearted things.

Willie Lynch wanted Blacks to completely turn their backs on themselves and their communities. He trained them to only be loyal to them, their money, their clothing stores, their banks, their cars. The Black race is to a point where we'd prostitute (sell our soul and our people) ourselves for materials. Things (possessions) reign supreme over unity in the streets, because we have been programmed to have a 'fuck them other niggas' mentality. Most of us don't understand or see the destruction, internally or externally, of selfish 'I gotta get mine' thought patterns. There's nothing wrong with handling your business and getting on your grind if you don't become oppressive with it, stepping on the necks of people in the illusion that it's prosperity.

FOLLOWING FAILURE

The idiocy of following behind an ideology of males (Larry Hoover, David Barksdale, Willie Lorde, and many others) who miserably failed in life plagues mindless Black bodies. They are unable to be their own man, stand on their own two feet, and think for themselves. They need another male to govern them, telling them what they can and cannot do. They allow males who don't represent manhood, males who try and spit knowledge from the teachings, but live corrupt and savage in their actions dictate their life. Hypocrites in the purest form.

These gang chiefs and leaders are not men of honor. They don't live in the highest moral principles or the absence of deceit or fraud. There can be no honor amongst people who are not living honorably in life. A person's mind and heart must be led by integrity in order to be a man of honor, and the toxic bloodline that runs to the heart of gangs is led by hatred and stupidity that's masked by an illusion of honor. A pile of shit with sugar on it is still a pile of shit.

ANALYZE

You have to ask yourself what success has come from being part of an organization? What success has come from living in a destructive hopeless existence (being locked up, shot, trapped in the confinements of the hood, and not living out your full potential)? Young fools (gang members) turn into old fools (gang members) who most of the time still operate on the same malfunctional level they did when they were young. The ones who do prosper did so after denouncing the gang they were a part of. They came to the realization of how foolish and stupid it is to be a part of a group that retardates the growth of the mind from a boyish state into manhood.

What is your value? Really analyze your answer because claiming an organization is re-enslavement, and it shows you have no value of yourself whatsoever. You can't respect, honor, or cherish the existence that is you because you are choosing to live in a suicidal realm. The Gangster Disciples, Stones, Vice Lords, Four Corner Hustlers, Crips, and all the other ones don't care about you. You are a momentary asset that can easily become disposed of. The pseudo-love a gang has for you is conditional, because once you begin to think on your own you are useless to the structure. You become of no use because you are walking your own path and coming to your own conclusions. Discover your value and live out your true identity. Your purpose and worth are waiting on you, and it has nothing to do with following the detrimental ideology of males who failed.

CHAPTER 5:
THE ATTACK ON THE BLACK RACE

THE NEW SLAVE

From the beginning of what we know as America the Black man, Black woman, and Black child have been hated and maliciously attacked. It began with chattel slavery, which placed the Black body in the status of property. It then went to Jim Crow, which put Blacks in an inferior status of a second-class citizen. In the present, it's the prison industrial complex, which is chattel slavery (ownership of human beings), and Jim Crow all wrapped up in one.

The creation of the felon has been the best form of the reinvention of the slave. It has the illusion that it is colorblind and majority of people, Black and White, support it, unconscious to the similarities of the inmate and convict to the slave. Black males in this country only make up 6% of the population, but account for over half of the prison population. Their identity, family, true freedom, civil rights have been wiped away, erased. Felons are walking numbers inside and outside of prison, second-class citizens whose life can be infringed upon anytime the justice system feels like it.

The prison system is big business, just like slavery was big business. The people who constructed the new form of the slave (the felon) knew by corrupting the mind with gangs, materialistic views, drugs, guns, and chaos the body would fall into the trap of incarceration. The 13th Amendment clearly states what is happening in the present:

"Section 1: Neither slavery nor involuntary servitude, except as a punishment for crime whereof the party shall have been duly convicted, shall exist within the United States, or any place subject to their jurisdiction."

The government implemented racially biased plans that would keep the Black man, Black woman, and Black child under their control - prisons, inadequate schools, and ghettos. A prison compound is similar to a slave compound. The prisoner experiences some of the things the slave did, like division from family. When a person is sent to prison they are usually shipped hundreds of miles away from their family, phone calls are set at prices people can't afford, and eventually the family bond crumbles. Inside prison there is forced labor where if you don't do what they say you can be sent to segregation or some other form of punishment. Education is limited, and they ban certain books and information that empowers one's self to gain the true knowledge of who they are, just like they did in the time of slavery.

The faces of racism have transformed many times, from chattel slavery to Jim Crow laws, racial policies, redlining practices in urban cities, the killing of Black people by the police, mass incarceration, the 100:1 ratio crack law that was in effect, defunding of Black schools, and many other things that keep Blacks trapped. Racist people will never cease to exist, that is the foundation that has been built under the world.

And as Black people we have a tendency to feed the beast, helping to keep the race in a feeble status.

PROGRAMMING

The puppet masters who sit at the head of the table (elite whites) even control what is being fed to our mind (subconscious) through the music and programs we take in. They have a deep understanding of how powerful subliminal messaging is to the psyche. They use ignorant money-hungry niggas as a medium to corrupt the psyche of the youth to only aspire to have a foreign car, wear designer clothes, be tough, pop bottles, and fuck on plenty of women. On the flipside, young girls only desire to be thick, catch a dude with plenty of money, and wear designer clothes because this is what society is telling them they need to have in order to be relevant, happy and of substance.

In the mid 80's into the early 90's, the Black community saw a conscious movement that looked as if it was going to bring the unconscious Blacks back to Blacks with pride. Hip-Hop was manifesting a reconnection within the hearts of its listeners to the knowledge of themselves. Reality rappers like Public Enemy, 2-Pac, the early N.W.A., De La Soul, Rakim and Eric B, Poor Righteous Teachers, Queen Latifah, and many others were spitting knowledge, wisdom, and understanding through the mic. Even their names, the titles they seen themselves by, were esteemed (KRS-1 'Knowledge Reign Supreme', Grandmaster Flash, Rakim Allah, and many others). These masters of ceremony were taking brothers and sisters in the ghetto to school, giving them transformative knowledge, true education.

Divide & Conquer

When the white racist powers at the top of the record labels and distribution companies took notice of the powerful conscious movement that was happening they quickly shut it down. They ushered in gangsta rap (street niggas glorifying false illusions of becoming rich selling drugs, making a name by killing people, and degrading the womb).

Gangsta rap brought in sexist views, glorification of chaos, gang bangin', and other detrimental things. It turned the dial of young minds from being conscious, building on knowledge, wisdom, and understanding to ghetto zombies who only wanted to get high, sell drugs, and regress into a state of savagery. During the years of gangsta rap, the murder rates shot through the roof, the drug trade exploded, which made mass incarceration (enslavement of Black bodies) justified.

The Black youth didn't want to be upright men and women of honor who were builders. They wanted to be the Nino Browns, the O-Dogs, the Kanes, the Dough Boys, the Scarfaces; fictitious characters who were either killed or imprisoned. Like in the song *"Ghetto Heroes"* by *Master-P* he says, *"Air Jordan ain't no muthafuckin' hero G, my heroes is niggas in the ghetto that slang D, that ride on golds and triple golds, and pimp hoes, and take any nigga in the click to the Super Bowl."* That rhyme is the mentality of unconscious males and females in the ghetto. This mind frame is learned through subliminal influences. Those gangsta rhythms were their mother, father, and teacher. It made them want to live that lifestyle that unconscious rappers were bragging about even though a large majority of them had never sold drugs, shot a person, and didn't even live in the ghetto. They lived in big beautiful homes and got fat checks to glorify the street life to a person who didn't know any better.

Gangsta rap enforced the criminalization of the Black image, criminals, crackheads, prostitutes, gangbangers, niggas. It made it that much easier to be afraid of them, to kill them, and to incarcerate them. The proof is evident once you open your mind to the trap that has been set. Gangsta rap brought a form of pride in being a dope boy, a hood nigga, a fool, a nigga that get down on his own people, a follower, and a consumer who loves to be taken (buying materials that are cheaply made with high price tags).

They (white elites) want the Black race to become extinct on a mental level, and the tactics that has been put into place has been working extremely well. A lot of young and older Black minds are only focused on getting money, and the valueless materials that come with it. Having morals, values, being stand-up, having self-respect, self-love don't mean nothing if it doesn't make money. This thought pattern has caused them to lose self in the midst of chasing, dying, and selling their soul for materials.

KNOWLEDGE

The education systems in Black communities are poisoning our Black babies with skills on how to take tests to please the state. They're learning informational education instead of transformational education. In white school districts, they teach and invest in their children, giving them life skills on how to be self-sufficient, entrepreneurs, leaders, innovators, thinkers, and people who are not afraid to go after success. They have economical programs, financial literacy courses, science programs, and an array of other classes that aid in expanding the mind. In the ghetto, the school systems teach Black students irrelevant knowledge that doesn't aid them whatsoever in a healthy successful life. Blacks learn how to be great mediocre employees.

Willie Lynch said in his letter that, "language was a peculiar institution". He said that, "The more a foreigner (a Black person) knows about the language of the land the more he or she is able to move through all levels of that society." Let's breakdown the word peculiar. This means belonging to some group or thing. The definition of language falls in the category of a linguistical system. What he was saying is their systems of the financial spectrum, the political spectrum, the justice system, and the educational system is only meant for them to understand. A small minority of the Black race caught on to the power of the language in these fields and prospered from it.

The Black school systems fail to teach Blacks the language of the land, which sends them out into the world with major disadvantages. They don't have an understanding about how the world works and their position in it. They come out of school with an inferior survival complex because they were never taught the language of themselves, the language of innovation, economies, prosperity in all realms, enlightened entrepreneurship, family, and many other linguistics. Blacks were given the language of chaos, regression, and mental death. Willie Lynch said, *"If you teach a slave the language (the system), he will know all your secrets, and then he is no more a slave, for you can't fool him any longer, and a fool is one of the basic ingredients to the maintenance of the slavery system."*

In 1984, President Ronald Wilson Reagan told the American people (white people) that he was going to get tough on crime and used the slogan "Let's Make America Great Again". The declaration was code words (a language) that meant he was going to bring the hammer down on the Black race, which he did. During his presidency, 1981-1989, the Black community experienced extreme poverty, Black bodies were being incarcerated at alarming rates, drugs and guns flooded the hood, racist policies blocked Blacks from free America, and chaos became a normalcy in the ghetto. When President William Jefferson Clinton signed the 'Crime Bill' and backed it with thirty billion dollars to fight the war on crime (the war against Blacks) the incarceration rate rose by 2000%. What has happened and is still happening is not some delusional attack or some crazy conspiracy theory. The proof is evident out in the streets, in the cages that hold Black bodies, in the minds of hood niggas, dope boys, and pimps.

A person can never truly understand themselves until they analyze where their thoughts and beliefs stem from. You may believe your thought patterns, characteristics, and beliefs are your own, but they are not. Everything you know and believe you have been programmed to believe it. You have to put yourself under your mental microscope and figure out, WHO YOU ARE? When you become your own man, you have your own core values that represents who you are. You build on your knowledge, live in the wisdom of your destiny, while gaining understanding of your purpose.

Divide & Conquer

CHAPTER 6:
WAKE UP

OPEN YOUR EYES

Why is it important to have a deep understanding of what Willie Lynch taught? For one, he and people like him created disorganization of the race, which caused us to go against the Law of Nature. Any species that are not organized (to form as or into a whole consisting of interdependent or coordinated parts especially for harmonious or united action) are doom for annihilation and extinction. The destruction of the Black mind effects every Black person that's alive in the moment, and it will cripple every Black person that's to come.

Why should you care? For a lot of people, the past means nothing to them because they are unconscious to its connection to the future. You should care because the disease of niggerism is hereditary, the Willie Lynch Syndrome is hereditary, meaning it is passed down from generation to generation. The ignorance, foolishness, and stupidity of what's going on out in the streets is why you should care. The drug trade is destroying Blacks in the illusion of riches, pimps are putting the woman back into the status of a piece of property, gangs and organizations bring false importance and power. The Black man, Black woman, and Black child is dying mentally and out in the streets, and it's becoming a normalcy, a way of life.

You should be disturbed because generations have been trained, taught, and programmed to have a 'fuck them other niggas' mentality. Blacks have been taught to say fuck themselves and love the illusion of the White man's wealth becoming mentally weak and dependent on materials to make them feel relevant. It's vital that you become aware that the street nigga's mentality is a stunt in natural growth.

Right now, in this moment, you are who you are because of the events that took place in the environment around you. Everything that you know and believe is inside of you because it was taught to you, and you either consciously or unconsciously embraced it. No Black child is born into this world with aspirations to grow up in a blanket of niggerism, mental corruption or hopeless ambitions. Every destructive belief (dope dreams, sexist views, gang life, etc.) was placed into your subconscious, and since it was a learned behavior it can be unlearned if you desire to live out the essence that brings life to your being.

MEDICINE

To correct the indoctrination of the teachings of Willie Lynch's 'fuck them other niggas' mentality and other detrimental belief systems you must kill the nigga within and let the Black man, Black woman, and Black child live. You must saturate yourself in self-discovery practices, and gain the true knowledge of who you are. Understand and analyze your foundation. Who are you? What do you stand for? What do you represent? What are your values and morals? If all you know how to do is fight, sell drugs, manipulate a woman, and be a brainless hood nigga you are lost. You are primitive in your development.

You are a Black man, a Black woman, or Black child then represent what that means. It comes with huge responsibilities, unlike that of the nigga. Black people have a duty to each other, the race, and the community. Duties that entail cultural, spiritual (not religious), and financial education that is transformational. We must be teachers to all, walking in the wisdom of an upright role model, being reliable, and respectable to the highest standard. The Black race is not represented by hood niggas, gang bangers, pimps, or dope fiends. Those toxic mentalities were taught to operate in their lowest self, but you have the power to tap into and recognize the supreme essence that is in you, and that is you.

A lot of people who are mentally blind can't connect that the things of one's past materializes their reality in the present. It is of no importance to them to know about a bunch of dead people that did things that don't seem like much in the now to their limited minds that only want to get money, ride slick, and be popular. They don't comprehend their connection to them. If there hadn't been a David Walker, a W.E.B. Du Bois, a William Ferris, a Marcus Garvey, an Ida B. Wells, a Malcolm X, and plenty of other people the nation would have probably never came out of Jim Crow or chattel slavery. As Black people we should pay homage through upright actions to the people, well known and unknown, that had the heart to speak out and fight. They fought not only for their generation, but for the generations that came behind them.

Gaining the knowledge of yourself so you can develop into a Black man or Black woman of substance means you must search your core down to the nucleus.   It means you must understand the ingredients (people) that make up you. If any of those ingredients are infected with the Willie Lynch Syndrome you have to analyze why they are there, then ask yourself is the niggerism hurting or helping you? You already know the answer to this if you are being real with yourself.

LOOKING IN THE MIRROR

The Willie Lynch Syndrome keeps the Black mind in a state of confusion and disconnected from its supreme essence. It is vital that you see the man or woman you were before you put on the mask of a street nigga, a goon, a pimp, or savage life. Who is that guy or girl that shows her or his face in the moments of solitude?

The brain is the most powerful tool there is. It is supreme in nature and one with the universe. Everything wonderful and amazing is innately in you. One thing the brain is able to do is correct itself if it taps into one's essence, your (our) historic original base. Willie Lynch understood the significance a person's culture and heritage played in their growth. Having the correct image of self is empowering, it brings about pride in one's self and race.

The connection of one's culture, heritage, and respect had to be cut off, or as he said, "Shave off a brute's mental history and create a multiplicity of phenomena of illusions (dope boy dreams, gang success), so that each illusion will twirl in its own orbit." He's talking about the illusion that many Black people have taken as their truth, the inferiority complex, being savage, being a nigga, being a thug, and having a poverty mentality.

If a people is pushed far enough in a hopeless state, one of two things will occur, either a strength that's unstoppable will be borne or they will stop giving a fuck. In the present, the adults are living in this state of not giving a fuck, which is teaching the younger generation to not give a fuck. If doesn't nobody care or a small number of people within the race care that leaves us vulnerable to police killings, Black bodies being hoarded into prisons, consumer exploitation, housing exploitation, and the stupidity of gangs.

Energy is life whether you dedicate it to negativity or positivity. The question is why would you want to waste your energy on negativity, things (activities) that don't produce any fruit? It takes a lot of energy to live upright and follow the path you aim to walk, but people fail to realize it takes the same amount of energy, if not more, to build on negative actions and thoughts. Your energy is your power, it's your thoughts, your desires. It is what makes your heart pump, and so why invest this supreme source into frivolousness?

The Black community has enormous power that is lying dormant. A power that can bring true wealth in all realms to the whole instead of just the individual. It makes no logical sense why one of the most powerful races is in a state of destruction, blinded by materials, drugs, and stupidity. Willie Lynch and people like him have been engraining in our minds for hundreds of years division, self-hatred, and a complacency of an inferior existence. As a race, we must embrace the rebirth of our self-image, build on 'each one, teach one', form toxic-free unity, self-love, and wake up to the greatness of the universe that resides inside of us.

CHAPTER 7:
BECOMING OF THE RACE

CHOICES

You can choose whether you are going to live your life as a nigga or as a beautiful Black person. What does being Black represent? Black, in all the shades that it comes in is divinity, it's something to be praised and proud of. It represents esteem, respect, honor, and dignity. As a member of the race who is stand-up and upright you have duties and responsibilities to its elevation, meaning you must be the vanguard, contesting anything that goes against the ascending of the race (gangs, hood niggas, dope boys, pimps). Remaining silent to the decimation makes you also a part of the problem.

What does it mean to gain the knowledge of yourself and the world around you? It means that you understand, grasping the significance and importance of who you were meant to be culturally, individually, and spiritually. There are Black people wandering around the ghetto, lost, and they don't care because the only thing they understand is getting money, partying, riding slick, and dressing fresh. Finding self is done through cultivation of the mind, feeding it healthy foods, and having a desire to destroy the cycle; stepping out of the mental prison you were placed in. When you know who you are you get rid of all the masks that you hid under, revealing your true identity. Materials won't need to be present to make you feel of importance.

Knowing thy self is recognizing that you are interconnected and interdependent upon more things than just yourself. No one is a self-made organism. You stand on the shoulders of many men and women who dedicated their lives and gave their lives to make a better world in their present and for future generations. You are part of a generational community whether you want to embrace it or not. By living blinded you are failing yourself and everyone you are connected to, your parents, your children, and your community.

When you step into the light through a mental cultivation rebirth you destroy the destructive nigga mind frame. Productivity becomes a part of your DNA make-up. The first steps in doing this is by changing your thoughts, which will produce better actions, release positive energy. Your thoughts and beliefs manifest everything that is happening in your life, and if you want to change your circumstances then work on your thinking and the way you view yourself. When you become conscious of how supreme you are, eliminating the 'fuck them other niggas' mentality, you will begin to live out your purpose and the pieces of your existence will fall into place.

PEACE & LOVE

Salvation is a must in your mental resurrection from niggerism to upright Blackness. When I use the term salvation by no means am I encouraging a religious connection. A lot of religions teach and practice hate, separatism, sexual bias, and are discriminatory if you don't convert to their belief system. Only you can save yourself, no holy book or so-called prophet is going to bring true peace to your life, your heart, or mind. Don't bet on false hope when you have all the answers lying dormant inside of you.

Finding yourself means you care about your life. People who care about themselves do productive things, they raise their children in that same light, and they constantly build on knowledge, wisdom, and understanding constructing a culture of power while equalizing themselves to their divinity. Niggas build on destruction, chaos, and they teach their children how to be niggas, ignorant, uneducated, and primitive. When you properly nourish your mind, your seed (offspring) benefits, your family benefits, and the people around you benefit because you are setting a model, a standard.

Cooperation and love amongst each other is vital for healthy growth, especially within your own community. Black people with nigga mentalities have to make the transition into Black men, Black women, and Black children, shedding off the stupidity of toxic teachings and beliefs. Kill off the moronic gang mentality, the broke ass drug dealer fantasies, the bird brain hood nigga, and extract the person you were meant to be, the righteous parent, sibling, role model, friend, partner, and human being. The reality of the matter is we are all of the same essence, Black, White, Latino, Asian, etc.

Productivity also represents accountability for yourself and the people within your community. Your family and your friends need to be able to rely on you. Your word needs to be your bond, and your actions need to match up with everything you profess. You can't be the male who claims to love his kids or freedom but is back and forth to jail because he involves himself in cancerous activities. When you step into manhood or womanhood, you are responsible, you have a duty to be the best version of you that you can possibly be. Is it going to be hard? Hell yeah, because it's new, unfamiliar. However, nothing is worth having in life without struggle. The struggle brings about strength, resilience.

OBLIGATIONS

When you become the master of yourself and break away from the brainwashing that has taken place you become a teacher, a valuable person filled with jewels. You stop worshipping bullshit, street niggas, gang creed, the drug trade, and many other false representations of manhood and power. You start to teach the people, especially the little ones, what Black represents. You have a pure mind, clear visions, and self-worth. You see the beauty in yourself no matter if you have a million dollars to your name or fifty cents.

The Black community has to bring the neighbor back to the hood. How can this be done? By simply caring about what goes on in your community and holding the traders (niggas) accountable. Invest in your neighborhood by keeping it clean, weeding out the stupidity and having each other's back. You can change your environment by putting your foot down and setting a model that eventually others will follow.

You cannot just sit back in a helpless state like you don't have the power to make a difference.

Detoxing your mind from the Willie Lynch Syndrome means you also have to detox the effects of that mentality within your neighborhood. Become the caretaker of the area you call home. If the neighborhood looks filthy, then organize a clean-up day for the community, and build a beautification program that becomes repetitive. If your neighborhood is peppered with abandoned or run-down houses, either buy them, fix them and sell them or call the city and have them torn down. Hold the people (your children, brothers, cousins, grandchildren) whose selling drugs, shooting each other, running hoe houses, and bringing chaos to your abode accountable. It's not on the government, the church, or the mosque to correct where you live, it's on you.

Recognize the cancers and awaken them to the path the community is going towards or eliminate them with all parties involved. Let it be known that no nonsense will be accepted or tolerated in your community. Like I said before, these niggas who are killing kids, polluting your area with drugs and causing chaos are your kin, family, and friends. You have the power to change your environment and rid it of the parasitic mind frame that is eating away at the empowerment movement of the race.

CULTURE

We have to create a new culture, because we have adopted one of pure destruction out of fear, out of a false image of self. We must analyze ourselves, not caring what anybody thinks, and shed off all characteristics and attributes that stem from niggerism. Why is it important? Just think about how ridiculous it is to be proud to be a nigga, praise and be willing to risk your life for the ideology of another man who failed in life, or aspire to be a dope boy or a pimp. Niggas embrace being ignorant, primitive, and uneducated, which is insanity when you have a tool of the essence with so much power sitting in your head. The human mind is supreme and unstoppable when it is activated.

This book is not some type of philosophy where I expect everybody to hold hands and sing "We Are the World". Naw, not at all. What I want you to realize is the generational programming that took place that has Black males and Black females living out a culture of retardation in the present, gangs, drugs, and violence. I know the reality of some is that they are going to be good little niggas and kill other Black people over petty disputes, push toxins in their community to fill their low self-esteem with overpriced materials, and love everything about that detrimental lifestyle. However, due to the fact that you are reading this book means that you are either conscious to what is going on and are increasing your mental functions to the reality, or you are at a crossroad in your life where you are realizing the hood nigga image you have been living probably most of your life has brought you many failures and downfalls.

It's time, right now in this moment, to become an upright Black man, Black woman, and Black child breaking the 'fuck them other niggas' mentality. A mind frame that in all actuality is saying fuck yourself. You cannot love yourself, but hate your own. Learn who you truly are, and build on that daily. Study the man or woman that's under the mask and build your foundation, a platform that you can be proud of. A stage that is not tainted by mental engineering.

White and some Black people in society told us that we were second-class citizens, niggas, lazy, savages, criminals, and worthless. Some of us took these things and lived them out making what they said we were our reality. They taught us to see our Black women (the womb we come from) as bitches, hoes, and economics; distorting our minds on self before we were even birthed. We have to unlearn the lies and gain understanding, see things for what they truly are, and not for what they appear to be. We are, if we live as our true self, honorable, respectable, righteous, priceless Black men and Black women. Your heart pumps letting you know the divinity that flows through your body, release it, and start building instead of destroying.

In solidarity,

Knowledge Borne

Divide & Conquer

THE INFAMOUS "WILLIE LYNCH LETTER"

This speech was delivered by a white slave owner, William Lynch in 1712. The message is still true...

Gentlemen, I greet you here on the bank of the James River in the year of our Lord one thousand seven hundred and twelve. First, I shall thank you, the gentlemen of the Colony of Virginia, for bringing me here. I am here to help you solve some of your problems with slaves. Your invitation reached me on my modest plantation in the West Indies, where I have experimented with some of the newest and still the oldest methods for control of slaves. Ancient Rome would envy us if my program is implemented. As our boat sailed south on the James River, named for our illustrious King, whose version of the Bible we cherish, I saw enough to know that your problem is not unique. While Rome used cords of wood as crosses for standing human bodies along its highways in great numbers, you are here using the tree and the rope on occasion.

I caught the whiff of a dead slave hanging from a tree a couple miles back. You are not only losing valuable stock by hangings, you are having uprisings, slaves are running away, your crops are sometimes left in the fields too long for maximum profit, you suffer occasional fires, your animals are killed. Gentlemen, you know what your problems are; I do not need to enumerate your problems, I am here to introduce you to a method of solving them. In my bag here, I have a fool proof method for <u>controlling your black slaves. I guarantee everyone of you that if installed correctly will control the slaves for at least 300 hundred years.</u> My method is simple. Any member of your family or your overseer can use it.

I have outlined a number of differences among the slaves, and *I take these differences and make them bigger.* I use <u>distrust</u> and <u>envy</u> for control purposes. These methods have worked on my modest plantation in the West Indies and it will work throughout the South. Take this simple little list of differences, and think about them. On top of my list is "Age", but it is there only because it starts with "A", the second is "Color" or shade, there is *intelligence, size, sex, size of plantations, status* on plantations, attitude of owners, whether the slaves live in the valley, on a hill, East, West, North, South, have fine hair, coarse hair, or is tall or short.

Now that you have a list of differences, I shall give you an outline of action, but before that, I shall assure you that distrust is stronger than trust, and envy is stronger than adulation, respect, or admiration. The Black slave after receiving this introduction shall carry on and will become self-refueling and self-generating for hundreds of years, maybe thousands.

Don't forget you must pitch the old Black male vs. the young Black male, and the young Black male against the old Black male.

You must use the dark skin vs. the light skin slaves, and the light skin slaves vs. the dark skin slaves.

You must use the female vs. the male, and the male vs. the female. You must also have your white servants and overseers distrust all Blacks, but it is necessary that your slaves trust and depend on us. They must love, respect and trust only us. Gentlemen, these kits are your keys to control.

Use them. Have your wives and children use them, never miss an opportunity. If used intensely for one year, the slaves themselves will remain perpetually distrustful.

Thank you gentlemen,

Willie Lynch

Divide & Conquer

[WHAT FOLLOWS ARE LYNCH'S INSTRUCTIONS ON MAKING A SLAVE:]

<u>Let us make a slave.</u> What do we need? First of all we need a black nigger man, a pregnant nigger woman and her baby nigger boy. Second, we will use the same basic principle that we use in breaking a horse, combined with some more sustaining factors. What we do with horses is that we break them from one form of life to another, that is, we reduce them from their natural state in nature; whereas nature provides them with the natural capacity to take care of their needs and the needs of their offspring, we break that natural string of independence from them and thereby create a dependency state, so that we may be able to get from them useful production for our business and pleasure. Cardinal Principles for Making a Negro fear that our future generations may not understand the principles of breaking both of the beast together, the nigger and the horse. We understand that short range planning economics results in periodic economic chaos; so that, to avoid turmoil in the economy, it requires us to have breath and depth in long range comprehensive planning, articulating both skill sharp perception. We lay down the following principles for long range comprehensive economic planning.

1. Both horse and nigger are no good to the economy in the wild or natural state.

2. Both must be broken and tied together for orderly production.

3. For orderly futures, special and particular attention must be paid to the female and the youngest offspring.

4. Both must be crossbred to produce a variety and division of labor.

5. Both must be taught to respond to a peculiar new language.

6. Psychological and physical instruction of containment must be created for both. We hold the six cardinal principles as truth to be self-evident, based upon the following, the discourse concerning the economics of breaking and tying the horse and nigger together, all inclusive of the six principles laid down above.

Accordingly, both a wild horse and a wild or natural nigger is dangerous even if captured, for they will have the tendency to seek their customary freedom, and in doing so, might kill you in your sleep. You cannot rest. They sleep while you are awake and are awake while you are asleep. They are dangerous near the family house and it requires too much labor to watch them away from the house. Above all, you cannot get them to work in this natural state. Hence, both the horse and the nigger must be broken; that is break them from one form of mental life to another, keep the body, take the mind! In other words, break the will to resist.

Now the breaking process is the same for both the horse and the nigger, only slightly varying in degrees. But as we said before, there is an art in long range economic planning. You must keep your eye and thoughts on the female and the offspring of the horse and the nigger.

Knowledge Borne

A brief discourse in offspring development will shed light on the key to sound economic principles. Pay little attention to the generation of original breaking but **concentrate of future generation**. Therefore, if you break the female mother, she will break the offspring in its early years of development, and when the offspring is old enough to work, she will deliver it up to you, for her normal female protective tendencies will have been lost in the original breaking process.

For example, take the case of the wild stud horse, a female horse and an already infant horse and compare the breaking process with two captured nigger males in their natural state, a pregnant nigger woman with her infant offspring. Take the stud horse, break him for limited containment. Completely break the female horse until she becomes very gentle, whereas you or anybody can ride her in comfort. Breed the mare and the stud until you have the desired offspring. Then you can turn the stud to freedom until you need him again. Train the female horse whereby she will eat out of your hand, and she will in turn, train the infant horse to eat out of your hand also.

When it comes to breaking an uncivilized nigger, use the same process; but vary the degree and step up the pressure, so as to do a complete reversal of the mind. Take the meanest and most restless nigger, strip him of his clothes in front of the female, and the nigger infant, tar and feather him, tie each leg to a different horse faced in opposite directions, set him a fire and beat the horses to pull him apart in front of the remaining niggers. The next step is to take a bull whip and beat the remaining nigger male to the point of death, in front of the female and the infant. Don't kill him, but put the fear of God in him, for he can be useful for future breeding.

The breaking process of the African woman the female and run a series of tests on her to see if she will submit to your desires willingly. Test her in every way, because she is the most important factor for good economics. If she shows any sign of resistance in submitting completely to your will, do not hesitate to use the bull whip on her to extract that last bit of bitch out of her. Take care not to kill her, for in doing so, you spoil good economics. When in complete submission, she will train her offspring in the early years to submit to labor when they become of age.

Understanding is the best thing. Therefore, we shall go deeper into this area of the subject matter concerning what we have produced here in this breaking process of the female nigger. We have reversed the relationships. In her natural uncivilized state she would have a strong dependency on the uncivilized nigger male, and she would have a limited protective tendency toward her independent male offspring and would raise female offspring to be dependent like her. Nature had provided for this type of balance. We reversed nature by burning and pulling one civilized nigger apart and bull whipping the other to the point of death, all in her presence. By her being left alone, unprotected, with the male image destroyed, the ordeal caused her to move from her psychological dependent state to an independent state. In this frozen psychological state of independence, she will raise her male and female offspring in reversed roles. For fear of the young males' life, she will psychologically train him to be <u>mentally weak and dependent, but physically strong</u>. Because she has become psychologically independent, she will train her female offspring to be psychologically independent. What have you got? You've got the nigger woman out front and the nigger man behind and scared. This is a perfect situation for sound sleep and economies. Before the breaking process, we had to be alertly on guard at all times. Now we can sleep soundly, for out of frozen fear woman stands guard for us. He cannot get past her early infant slave molding process. *He is a good tool, now ready to be tied to the horse at a tender age.* By the time a nigger boy reaches the age of sixteen, he is soundly broken in and ready for a long life of sound and efficient work and the reproduction of a unit of good labor force.

Continually, through the breaking process of uncivilized savage niggers, by throwing the nigger female savage into a frozen psychological state of independence, by killing of the protective male image, and by creating a submissive dependent mind of the nigger male slave, we have created an orbiting cycle that turns on its own axis forever, unless a phenomenon occurs and re-shifts the positions of the male and female slaves. We show what we mean by example. Take the case of the two economic slave units and examine them closely.

The negro marriage unit we breed two nigger males with two nigger females. Then we take the nigger females away from them and keep them moving and working. Say the one nigger female bears a nigger female and the other bears a nigger male. Both nigger females, being without influence of the nigger male image, frozen with an independent psychology, will raise their offspring into reverse positions. The one with the female offspring will teach her to be like herself, independent and negotiable (we negotiate with her, through her, by her, and negotiate her at will). The one with the nigger male offspring, she being frozen with a subconscious fear for his life, will raise him to be mentally dependent and weak, but physically strong, in other words, body over mind. Now, in a few years when these two offspring's become fertile for early reproduction, we will mate and breed them and continue the cycle. That is good, sound, and long range comprehensive planning.

Warning: Possible

Interloping Negatives

Earlier, we talked about the non-economic good of the horse and the nigger in their wild or natural state; we talked out the principle of breaking and tying them together for orderly production. Furthermore, we talked about paying particular attention to the female savage and her offspring for orderly future planning; then, more recently we stated that, by reversing the positions of the male and the female savagaes, we had created an orbiting cycle that turns on its own axis forever, unless a phenomenon occurred and re-shifted the positions of the male and female savages.

Our experts warned us about the possibility of this phenomenon occurring, for they say that the mind has a strong drive to correct and re-correct itself over a period of time if I can touch some substantial original historical base, and they advised us that the best way to deal with the phenomena of illusions, so that each illusion will twirl in its own orbit, something similar to floating balls in a vacuum. This creation of a multiplicity of phenomena of illusions entails the principles of cross-breeding the nigger and the horse as we stated above, the purpose of which is to create a diversified division of labor thereby creating different levels of labor and different values of illusion at each connecting level of labor. The results of which is the severance of the points of original beginnings for each sphere illusion. Since we feel that the subject matter may get more complicated as we proceed in laying down our economic plan concerning the purpose, reason, and effect of cross-breeding horse and niggers, we shall lay down the following definition terms for future generations.

1. Orbiting cycle means a thing turning in a given path.

2. Axis means upon which or around which a body turns.

3. Phenomenon means something beyond ordinary conception and inspires awe and wonder.

4. Multiplicity means a great number.

5. Sphere means a globe.

6. Cross-breeding a horse means taking a horse and breeding it with an ass and you get a dumb backward ass long-headed mule that is not reproductive nor productive by itself.

7. Cross-breeding niggers means taking so many drops of good white blood and putting them into as many nigger women as possible, varying drops by the various tone that you want, and then letting them breed with each other until the circle of colors appear as you desire. What this means is this: Put the niggers and the horse is the breeding pot, mix some asses and some good white blood and what do you get? You got a multiplicity of colors of ass backward, unusual niggers, running, tied to backward ass long-headed mules, the other sterile. (The one constant, the other dying, we keep the nigger constant for we may replace the mule for another tool) both mule and nigger tied to each other, neither knowing where the other came from and neither productive for itself, nor without each other.

Controlled Language

Cross-breeding completed, for further severance from their original beginning, must completely annihilate the mother tongue of both the new nigger and the new mule and institute a new language that involves the new life's work of both. You know, language is a peculiar institution. It leads to the heart of a people. The more a foreigner knows about the language of another country the more he is able to move through all levels of that society. Therefore, if the foreigner is an enemy of the country, to the extent that he knows the body of the language, to that extent is the country vulnerable to attack or invasion of a foreign culture. For example, you take a slave, if you teach him all about your language, he will know all of your secrets, and he is then no more a slave, for you can't fool him any longer, and a fool is one of the basic ingredients to the maintenance of the slavery system.

Divide & Conquer

OTHER BOOKS BY KNOWLEDGE

FOUND ON: AMAZON - BARNES & NOBLE - KINDLE

Get On Your Grind - $10.95
ISBN-13: 978-1976169748
ISBN-10: 1976169747

Get On Your Grind is a jewel of enlightenment that will bring about a mental, emotional, and spiritual transformation and inner resurrection. It will show the unconscious how to reach redemption and succeed after imprisonment. The contents that reside in this book bring clarity and solutions to life's obstacles of being a felon out in the free world. It gives a person the tools on how to gain unrestricted freedom, building a solid foundation that will sustain the hardships and failed attempts that will come their way. This book is a must read for anybody who wants to rise above incarceration.

Divide & Conquer

Trapped - $14.95
ISBN-13: 978-1977817747
ISBN-10: 1977817742

An electrifying novel about a young black male named Benny Williams, a child of the ghetto who struggles to find himself in an environment where drug lords and street legends define the model of success. He navigates his way through the south side of Chicago, Illinois known as the Wild Hundreds; believing that getting money in the streets is the ultimate goal. He's mentally blinded, but conscious to certain aspects of the genocide going on in his community. Yet, he internally battles to relinquish the negativity of what he has been fed to believe; allowing his surroundings to mold his reality.

Divide & Conquer

ABOUT THE AUTHOR

Knowledge Borne was birthed in the city of Chicago in 1984. Growing up, he was an impressionable kid. He grew up in an environment that told him being hard and tough were the characteristics of what being a real man was. The illusion of power became intriguing to him (gangbangin', dope boy dreams, stick-up kid ambitions, and gettin' money), and before long he fell into the trap.

Through **Knowledge Borne's** many trials and tribulations he was able to take hold of his life and tap into the divine essence that lived inside of him. After his awakening he became determined to bring enlightenment to others through his words and his actions.

Knowledge Borne is passionate about mentally uplifting people, helping them gain the knowledge of themselves so that they can walk in their wisdom, and live in their understanding. He takes to heart his duty as a Poor Righteous Teacher.

Please contact **Knowledge Borne** at:

IAmKnowledgeBorne@gmail.com

Facebook.com/KnowledgeBorne

www.ingramcontent.com/pod-product-compliance
Lightning Source LLC
Chambersburg PA
CBHW060750260726
48660CB00002B/560